I'm Pressing On

By Liz Scott

Cover Created by Jazzy Kitty Publications

Logo Designs by Andre M. Saunders/Leroy Grayson

Editor/Poem by Anelda L. Attaway

© 2018 Liz Scott

ISBN 978-1-7324523-0-5

Library of Congress Control Number: 2018947739

All rights reserved. This book is protected by the copyright laws of the United States of America. This book may not be copied or reprinted for commercial gain or profit. The use of short quotations or occasional page copying for personal or group study is permitted and encouraged. Permission will be granted upon request. For Worldwide Distribution. Printed in the United States of America. Published by Jazzy Kitty Publications utilizing Microsoft Publishing Software. Scripture KJV.

ACKNOWLEDGMENTS

I want to first acknowledge God who is the Head of my life and the joy of my Salvation. I praise God for speaking the words to me in writing this book.

My mother Ellen Scott for having a strong united family.

A special thanks to my niece Anelda Attaway, CEO of Jazzy Kitty Publications for helping to make my dreams a reality.

DEDICATION

This book is dedicated to my son Brian Martin-Scott. I am so proud of you! You are an awesome young man and I love you with all my heart.

Also, to my two grandsons' Brian Martin-Scott Jr. and Yasir Anderson. You guys will always be in my heart.

Last but not least, to the ENTIRE Scott Family!

TABLE OF CONTENTS

Introduction	i
The Test Results	01
About My Mom	01
The McGown Family	03
About Mom and Dad	08
The Layaway	11
Grandma Hattie	15
Through the Years	18
19th Street	18
Club Family Affair	19
Canada	21
Toronto	21
Auburn, New York	24
Motown	26
Orlando, Florida (Disney World)	28
The Car	31
80th Birthday Celebration	33
Mom, Love of Elephants	36

Day Trip-Sight and Sound 38

So Many Memories 39

January 2006 39

Chemotherapy! 42

Radiation Treatment 46

Praise God from Whom All Blessings Flow 46

August 2018 Mom's 90th Birthday 47

Mom's Favorite Scripture 49

Mom, You Keep Pressing On! 51

About the Author 56

INTRODUCTION

This is the true story of a strong and courageous woman named Ellen Scott. It is a loving and heartwarming story; that is sometimes funny, sometimes sad, but always inspirational. This is a story of love, family, and Ellen's faith in God.

And as you read the pages of this book you will find the story of a survivor, not just a cancer survivor, but a survivor of life!

The Test Results

The year was 2006, it was a cold and blustery day in January. Mom and I was at her home when she received a call from her Gynecologist at Temple University Hospital.

The doctor said to Mom, "I have the lab results from the test that you were given, and I would like you to come to my office so that I can speak with you regarding the results." So, Mom and I went to Temple University Hospital and met with her doctor.

The doctor said, "The tests are not good, and I have a bit of bad news. The test reveals that you have uterine cancer, a very aggressive form of cancer."

I was absolutely SHOCKED, unable to speak or move. I just sat there staring at the doctor.

Then I said to myself, *"Did I just hear the doctor tell my mom, MY MOM, that she has CANCER?!!!"*

About My Mom

My mother Ellen Scott was born Ellen Williams on August 9, 1928 in Florence, South Carolina. Her nickname is Du'chee which is the name that my Southern family still uses today.

They often ask, "Liz how's Du'chee doing?"

Mom's faith in God was always strong. For at the tender age of 10-years-old, Mom contracted Typhoid Fever, a bacterial infection.

Mom had two brothers and one sister. Her siblings also contracted Typhoid Fever, but their infection cleared up in minimal time. But not so much with Mom, she was ill for months.

Physicians in the south in 1938 were not readily available for "colored folks." Due to this, many Black people that contracted Typhoid Fever had expired.

My grandfather affectionately known as Pappa, had a physician come to the house to care for Mom, but still yet, this bacterial infection stayed with her for months.

And it was a journey! Mom was unable to get out of bed and all of her beautiful long thick black hair fell out. There was a radio at Mom's house and at certain times of the day would play spiritual songs. Therefore, she would listen to the spiritual songs which told her of the goodness of the Lord and His grace and mercy.

Being that Mom could not get out of bed, she would ask my grandmother and her siblings (her sister Emma and two brothers

John and Bubba) to carry her over to the radio so that she could put her hands on it. She wanted to literally feel the Spirit of the Lord coming through the radio. Come On Somebody!

She was only 10-years-old, so, they did honor her request. And they would daily carry her over to the radio so that she could put her hands on the radio while listening to the Spiritual songs.

After a few months of being down, Mom finally got better and was able to get out of bed. However, when she tried to stand up her left foot would not touch the floor. For the Typhoid Fever had drawn her leg up so much so that it was now shorter than her right leg and she could not stand with both feet on the floor.

My Grandma Annie worked with my mom's leg daily to get it back to normal. Eventually, her leg grew back to its normal length and her foot was perfectly touching the floor. And now Mom was able to walk, run, and move about just as she did before contracting Typhoid Fever. In addition, all of her beautiful, thick, long black hair grew back and it was just as beautiful as it was before her bout with Typhoid Fever.

The McGown Family

At the age of 12, Mom was working in White people homes

and caring for their children. This one particular family that she worked for was the McGown family. To get to work Mom had to walk several miles daily to and from the McGown's family home. Her daily routine was to clean their home and take care of their two children; Mack who was six-years-old and baby Ellen that was two-years-old.

The McGown family loved Mom and always treated her with respect. This one particular day Mom had finished her work and was about to walk home, but there was a bad storm with strong wind and heavy rain.

Mrs. McGown said to Mom, "I can't let you walk home in this heavy rain. I'll drive you home."

As Mrs. McGown was driving she would ask Mom, "How much further?"

Mom would reply, "Oh just a little further down the road."

When Mrs. McGown finally arrived at mom's house she asked, "Ellen, you walk all this way back and forth every day?"

Mom said, "Yes."

Mrs. McGown replied, "This is too far for you to walk every day."

Then Mrs. McGown asked my Grandma Annie, "Can Ellen

come and live with us? We'll take real good care of her and she won't have to walk so far every day."

My Grandma Annie agreed to let Mom go and live with the McGown's. As promised, the McGown's took real good care of Mom; for they loved her and thought of her as part of the family. Mom ate the best of food and was dressed in the best of clothing.

Mack and baby Ellen loved Mom as well. At bedtime, Mrs. McGown would try to get baby Ellen to go to the bathroom and she wouldn't go. Therefore, they would get Mom to take baby Ellen to the bathroom and she would go every time. Mack and baby Ellen had a real connection with Mom.

One particular time, Mack went to the movies with some of his family members. The movie that was playing was titled, "Since You Went Away," and it had a sad ending.

Due to the movies sad ending, Mack cried and cried. When he came back home he immediately told Mom how sad the movie was and that he cried at the end of the movie.

Mom said, "Oh Mack, it's just a movie, don't cry."

A few days later, Mom went to see the movie and Mack waited up until she got home.

As soon as mom walked through the door Mack asked, "Ellen

did you cry? Did you cry Ellen?"

Mom replied, "Yes Mack, I did cry, it got to me too." And then she hugged Mack.

Mom stayed with the McGown's for three years. And at the age of 15, Grandma Annie told Mom she had to come home to help out with their restaurant. Mom was heartbroken that she would have to leave the McGown's home for she loved living there and she loved the McGown family (Mr. and Mrs. McGown, Mack, and baby Ellen) and they loved her as well.

MOM AND DAD

About Mom and Dad

Mom was around the age of 15 when she met my dad, Cleveland Scott. They started courting (Southern term for dating) and then got married in Florence, South Carolina on March 28, 1950. From the Union they were blessed with seven children. Their first four children Bo, Butch, Randy, and Robert were born in Florence, South Carolina and were delivered buy one of the best if not the best midwives in Florence County, my Grandma Annie Williams.

In 1952, my dad moved his family to Philadelphia, Pennsylvania because he wanted a better life for his family than what the south had to offer at that time.

My brother Tomie, myself, and Linda were born in Philadelphia, Pennsylvania. My brother Tomie was the first child that my mother gave birth to in the hospital. The nurses were trying to tell my mom what to do; like when to push and when not to push.

My mom said, "Oh, I know what to do and when to do it."

Then one of the nurses sarcastically replied, "Oh well, maybe we should let you do the delivery yourself then."

Mom quickly replied in a serious tone, "And I could do just

that, my mother is one of the best midwives there is, and she delivered all four my sons without a problem. So yes, nurse I know what to do," Mom weren't too pleased with the hospital the staff.

We have always been a close-knit family, mom and dad instilled in us at a very young age to always stick together and never fight amongst ourselves.

One of my mom's favorite saying was, "I DON'T CARE IF HELL FREEZES OVER YALL STICK TOGETHER." And we always have and always will.

Mom and Dad both worked outside of our home, Dad was in construction and Mom did domestic work. For a short period of time Mom did do factory work, but for the most part she worked at White people homes cooking, cleaning, and taking care of their children. To get to work, Mom would ride three buses daily to get to their homes.

Mom has always said, "I have worked for some good White people. I have always had a good relationship with them. White people just seem to like me and I have always gotten along with them very well."

The White people that Mom worked for were always giving

her all sorts of things for her and her family. They would give Mom clothes, furniture, and food. I can remember on some Thanksgivings Mom would have to work at their home serving their guest dinner while we waited for her to come home. We would be sitting with anticipation waiting for her to walk through the front door. When Mom would reach the door, our eyes would light up and we would run to greet her. Mom would be loaded down with bags of food that the family packed for her to take home. **And we would have our Thanksgiving dinner after all, we were beaming with joy and thankfulness.** Mom didn't have to work every Thanksgiving, so we had our mom to ourselves. Therefore, all-day we were anticipating Thanksgiving dinner and the house was smelling of turkey, stuffing, rice and gravy, macaroni and cheese, potato salad, candied yams, and desserts. We didn't eat like this just on Thanksgiving, we ate like this every Sunday. Mom would prepare a big home cook meal and she would make cakes from scratch. She made Pineapple, Coconut, Jelly, and Chocolate cakes. Mom would cook during the week as well after she got home from work, but our big meals were always on Sundays.

In addition, Mom always make sure that we had all that we

needed both at home and school. She took pride in dressing her children in fine clothing.

She would say, "All my children have nice clothes to wear." And we did, Mom make sure of that.

The Layaway

Speaking of clothing, Mom told me of a time when she had put some clothes on layaway; she was eight months pregnant at the time. She was pregnant with either Tomie, me, or Linda. I'm not sure who she was pregnant with, but anyway Mom asked my dad to go and pick up the clothes she had on layaway. When my dad went to get the layaway the store personnel told my dad that the layaway had lapsed due to non-payment and he couldn't get the layaway. So, my dad came back home and told Mom that they wouldn't let him get the clothes off layaway due to non-payment.

My mom said to Dad, "Well, what about the money I already paid on the layaway? Take me down to that store."

So, rocking and reeling at eight months and pretty big, Mom walked into the store.

She says to the manager, "My husband came here to get the

clothes that I had on layaway and you told him he couldn't get the layaway because of non-payment."

The managers said, "Yes, that's right."

Mom immediately replied, "Well, what about the money that I already paid on this layaway?"

The manager quickly responds, "Well, because the layaway has lapsed, any money paid on the layaway is non-refundable."

Mom looked at the manager and said in a firm stern voice, "I understand that the layaway has lapsed, and I can no longer get the clothes I had on layaway. I can even understand that you cannot give any cash refunds, but I paid money on his layaway and Damn it you gonna give me my money's worth!" All while banging on the counter.

The manager says with fear, "OK, OK, let her get what she want for the money that she already paid on the layaway."

Mom got her money's worth and then she Rocked and Reeled on out the store.

Now, don't let this little story about the layaway get you twisted. My dad was a big and strong man. He was big both in stature and personality. At any time, he could straighten people out as well, but he didn't know anything about layaways.

You see, my mom did all the shopping for our clothes, but Mom had asked Dad to go pick up the layaway. So, he was just doing what my mom asked.

MOM AND HER MOTHER, MIDWIFE, ANNIE WILLIAMS

MOTHER-IN-LAW, MRS. HATTIE SCOTT THOMAS "GRANDMA HATTIE"

Grandma Hattie

Mom also had a wonderful relationship with her Mother-in-Law, Mrs. Hattie Scott-Thomas. Their relationship was more like Mother and Daughter instead of Mother-in-Law and Daughter-in-Law. Grandma Hattie had the biggest heart ever. She had a way of making all of children and grandchildren feel like they were the most special people in the world.

Dad would always take us back to Florence, South Carolina so that we could visit with our Southern relatives, especially Grandma Hattie. Mom and Dad would even let us spend the entire summer down south, and we enjoyed every minute of our time spent down south.

I can remember sitting on the porch shelling peas with Grandma and being in the kitchen watching her as she prepared good ole down home southern meals, made from scratch of course.

One of Grandma's favorite pass times was playing SPADES. Grandma taught all of us how to play spades. I can see her right now just a laughing and laughing because her and her partner just 'SET' her opponents. Yes, we love playing spades and we still play whenever we have our family gatherings.

Grandma Hattie was a special, special, lady and she will forever be in our hearts. Continue to Rest in Peace Grandma Hattie. WE WILL LOVE YOU FOREVER!!

ELLEN'S SEVEN BLESSED CHILDREN

Top Row: Left to Right
BUTCH, RANDY, ROBERT, AND BO

Bottom Row: Left to Right
LINDA, TOMIE, AND LIZ

Through the Years

Through the years, Mom continued to work for "good White people" as she would say. She cleaned, cooked, and cared for their children.

In 1967, she was working for Dr. Kanest and his family that lived out in the suburbs. Mom was in the process of purchasing a home on 19th and Lehigh Avenue. Dr. Kanest came down to North Philadelphia from the suburbs to speak with the real estate agent so he could vouch for mom. He told the agent that Mom worked for him and that her credibility is outstanding, also she is very trustworthy.

"I am asking you to approve this mortgage for Mrs. Ellen Scott, for as long as she wants to, she will always have a job with me," said Dr. Kanest. Mom was approved for the mortgage and we moved to 19th and Lehigh Avenue in North Philadelphia.

19th Street

During this time, Whites and Blacks lived on 19th Street and our house was around the corner from Connie Mack Stadium. The back of our house faced the stadium so when there were baseball games, the back of our house would be lit up with all the lights from the ball field.

In addition, we could see the fly balls flying through the air and we could see some of the seating area of the stadium.

19th and Lehigh Avenue, there are so many memories; this is the house we grew up in, it was home and Mom was always there through it all. She was there daily preparing us for school, meeting with our teachers, and attended each of our graduations. Mom let us participate in extra-curricular activities including sports. Whatever we were interested in or involved with, Mom was always there. Most importantly, Mom supported and encouraged us to be all that we dreamed we could be.

Club Family Affair

Oh, did I mention traveling, all the trips that Mom took us on? Well, in the early 80s Mom formed a group called Club Family Affair. It was made up of family members and Mom was the President.

Mom used the services of travel agencies to put together the trips for Club Family Affair and we would have at least 48 people traveling with us. Even though everyone traveling with us were not blood relatives, they all felt like they were with family because it was truly "A Family Affair."

Mom would sell dinners on the weekends to generate money to cover the cost of the trip for her children, grandchildren, great-grandchildren, and the neighbors' children as well. The menu for Mom's dinners were fried chicken, barbecue chicken, fried fish, barbecue ribs, pig feet, and chitlins. The sides were greens, string beans, macaroni and cheese, potato salad, and cornbread. The desserts were delicious, carrot cake and sweet potato pies.

My brother Bo and his co-workers were a huge support of Mom selling the dinners. He worked for the Triangle Corporation located at E & Erie in Philadelphia. He would get approximately 40 orders for dinners that had to be delivered by 11 a.m. Friday morning. Bo would come to the house Thursday evening and place the orders. Mom, Linda, and myself got those dinners together and was on point.

At 10:40 a.m., we were pulling up to Triangle Corporation with the dinners in tack. Everyone was always happy and very pleased with their dinners.

Therefore, they would always ask, "When's the next time Mom would be selling dinners?"

The trips were not just a lot of fun and exciting, but very

educational as well. Some of the places that we visited were:

- Canada (Niagara Falls, Toronto, and Montreal)
- Auburn, New York
- Detroit, Michigan
- Disney World in Orlando, Florida.

Canada

Niagara Falls a beautiful sight to see. It has a Canadian and an American side. We liked viewing the Falls from the Canadian side, it was a little more beautiful. At night, the Falls would be lit up in all different colors. Simply Beautiful!

Toronto

Toronto is a bustling city. Out of the three cities Niagara Falls, Toronto, and Montreal, Toronto is the city that feels most like home in Philadelphia. It has lots of restaurants, lots of people walking up and down the sidewalk, and a booming night life. In addition, it is a very clean city; no graffiti, no trash on the streets. Just a lovely city!

CANADA

CANADA

Auburn, New York

Auburn, New York is where Harriet Tubman made her home. We had visited the Harriet Tubman's house where tours are scheduled daily. We also met Harriet Tubman's great-great niece. She is at Harriet Tubman's house daily and is a tour guide. Some of the artifacts in the home are the true artifacts that was originally in the home when Harriet Tubman lived there. The home has been restored a few times over the years.

What an incredible experience and an exciting time we had on this trip. To visit the home of Harriet Tubman was simply amazing. We also visited the grave site of Harriet Tubman for she was buried in Auburn, New York the place she called home.

HARRIET TUBMAN

Motown

In Detroit, Michigan we visited Hitsville; the home of Motown. We toured the studio where the Motown sound originated. Smokey Robinson and the Miracles, the Supremes, and the Temptations were just a few of the artists that recorded their first songs which were all hits from this studio.

While at the studio the tour guide chose three of us to perform as the Supremes and five men from our group to perform as the Temptations. What a great time we had!

MOTOWN

Orlando, Florida (Disney World)

And then there was Orlando, Florida the home of Disney World. We visited the park daily and we had multi passes that allowed us entrance into Magic Kingdom, Universal Studios, and the Epcot Center.

We also went to Disney World in the evening to see the Electrical Parade, what a spectacular sight to see. I don't know who had more fun, the children or the adults. You really do become a kid again at Disney World.

DISNEY WORLD

Until this day, people are still asking about our trips wanting to know if we are going to be doing any more of them. Everyone that traveled with Club Family Affair truly enjoyed themselves and we had wonderful times on the trips. We actually visited Canada and Orlando, Florida several times. Oh, such sweet memories, they will last forever.

In addition, to those amazing trips, Mom would also take us on day trips and short trips. We went to places like Atlantic City, Wildwood, and Willow Grove, PA. In Willow Grove there was an amusement park called Willow Grove Park that we went to.

On this one particular day, we were at the park and Mom said, "Oh, we better get ready to go because it looks like a storm is coming."

It was getting dark and the wind was picking up. So, we got in the car and Mom drove the car, taking back roads trying to make it home before the storm came. We made it home before the storm. Yes indeed, Mom handled that car.

The Car

Speaking of cars, I am reminded of the time when my brother Butch brought this nice car which was a Tornado.

One morning, he went out to get in his car and it was gone. The salesman from the car dealership had come in the middle of the night and reprocessed his car. So, Mom went out to the dealership with my brother.

They said to Butch, "John (that's his real name) how much are you going to pay on the tires today?"

Mom said, "Not a G** Damn Penny! Yall out here with your fast-talking self, you think if you say 20 words before he says one, you think you got someone you can take advantage of. WELL, NOT TODAY!"

I won't tell you all the things my mom said to the salesman that day, but after she said a few things the White women comes out of their cubicles to look at Mom.

Mom said, "What you looking at, acting like you ain't never heard these words before. You done heard that and much more." The women quickly ducked back into their cubicles.

Mom told the salesman, "You sitting behind that desk like you all bad or something. You come from behind that desk and I'll whip your ass because I believe I can beat a White man's ass."

Then Mom said to Butch, "Don't come out here to buy no

more cars from these crooks and tell everybody else not to come out here either." Mom takes care of business!!!

Mom also has a soft and gentler side as well and people just simply loves her. She is affectionately known as Mom, Mommy, Mother, and Nana. People that are not blood related calls my mom Mother or Nana. People that she meets just become like family.

I had one person ask me, "Is it OK if I call your mom Nana?" I said, "Sure it's OK."

So not only was her rapport with White people good, mostly everyone she came in contact with had love for her and they still love her today.

Mom has an equal balance of a strong yet gentle loving, nurturing, kind, patient, and unconditional love. Love that bears all things and endures all things; that's Mrs. Ellen Scott.

80th Birthday Celebration

In my family we love to have big celebrations; we celebrate birthdays, we have 4th of July cookouts, Thanksgiving and Christmas dinners. Give us a reason to celebrate and it's on. At our celebrations there is always plenty of food, fun, laughter, music, and of course dancing.

Now, if you want to see Mom put her thing down, then play "Love and Happiness" by Al Green; that is her jam!!!

Until this day, she will get up, lay her cane down, and start doing her thing. She does this dance that I try to do, but I can't do it like she does. I don't think anyone can. And she will dance the whole record through.

80^(TH) BIRTHDAY CELEBRATION

Mom, Love of Elephants

Mom also loved collecting elephants ranging in all sizes. Elephants so small that they could sit in the palm of your hand and elephants that were so large that it took two people to carry it.

Mom had collected over 500 elephants that were all beautiful. Whenever someone traveled to places they would always bring her an elephant back.

MOM LOVE OF ELEPHANTS

Day Trip-Sight and Sound

Another day trip that Mom did was to Sight and Sound in Lancaster, Pennsylvania. If you have never seen one of their plays, then I suggest that you truly try to make it to one of their shows. The things that they do in that theater is absolutely amazing. Sight and Sound shows are all Biblical plays. The play that we saw this particular time was "Daniel and the Lions Den."

Before the day of the trip we had everyone read the Book of Daniel so that they would know and understand the story of Daniel. Everything that takes place in the Book of Daniel, they performed on stage. They showed the following:

- Daniel Interpreting Dreams
- The Huge Golden Image
- Shadrach, Meshach, and (A bad negro) aka Abed nego
- The Hand Writing on the Wall
- Daniel and the Lions' Den

There are live animals throughout the entire production. The shows at Sight and Sound are spectacular. It's an event that is a must see. We also saw other productions there as well, but for me, Daniel was that all-time best production ever.

So Many Memories

Memories, Memories, Memories... All of these memories stretch from childhood to adulthood and will forever be treasured in our hearts. As you know, there were no hand book giving instructions on how to be a great mom. Mom just did it and did it well.

In some magazines they have a section that says, "Who Wore It Best?"

Well, if they had a section on being the greatest mom and asked the question, "Who Did It Best?" There you would see my mom's name, "Mrs. Ellen Scott" for she truly is the best!!!

January 2006

So here we are in January 2006, Mom and I are sitting in the doctor's office and we have just been informed that she has cancer. I am totally speechless and cannot utter a word. And without any hesitation, Mom says to the doctor, "OK Dr. so what do we do now?"

The doctor replied, "The first step would be surgery to remove the tumor, then chemotherapy, and then radiation."

We left the doctor's office and went to my mom's house.

When we came in the house, my brother Butch and my niece Rhondalynn were there.

Mom says to them, "We have some news to tell you," and then she said, "go ahead Liz." I am still speechless, I could not form my lips to utter the words that mom has cancer.

So, Mom said, "I have cancer."

My brother was just like I was; he was in shock, speechless, and my niece just slid down the wall to the floor in disbelief.

Then Mom said, "It's alright because whatever God allows is alright with me."

We told the rest of the family and everyone chimed in with their thoughts of what should be done and how. Our first thoughts were that we need a second opinion; not just go by what the doctor said, which was understandable. Therefore, we did venture out to get a second opinion.

When I was asked by the medical professionals, "Well, who is the doctor that she is currently seeing?"

And when I gave them Mom's doctor name they said, "He's pretty good. He practices at Temple and Fox Chase. He's the head doctor and trains the upcoming and the new doctors in his field." Mom didn't even know all of this about her doctor.

She just said, "I like my doctor, I trust my doctor, and I don't want no other second opinion. I'm going with my doctor." And so, the process begins.

Mom was scheduled for surgery on February 14, 2006. We were all at the hospital anxiously waiting for the doctor to come out and tell us how our mom was doing. It seemed like it took forever, for we wanted to know how Mom was.

FINALLY, the doctor came out and said, "The surgery went very well, and the tumor was intact."

He was able to remove the entire tumor and the cancer had not spread to her lymph nodes. He also said that Mom would still be a little drowsy, but we could go back and see her. We went into the recovery room and like the doctor said Mom was a little drowsy, but she said that she was in pain. So, we asked the nurse to give her something and she did.

Mom looked good considering she had just came through surgery. Therefore, once she was admitted to her room, we left to let her get some rest.

Mom healed from the surgery very well. Within a months' time, the incision had completely healed. There was no scar nor any scar tissue, no nothing. In fact, if Mom hadn't shown you where the incision was you would not have known that she even had surgery.

Mom knew what she was talking about was she said she was going to have her doctor do the surgery and she didn't want to talk about getting a second opinion because her doctor did an awesome job with Mom's surgery. So, all is well, the surgery is completed, the tumor is removed, and Mom is looking and feeling great!!!

Chemotherapy!

We are now at step two in this process CHEMOTHERAPY! Being that Mom was 78-years-old at the time, her doctor didn't want to overwhelm her system with the chemotherapy treatments. So, Mom had to be hospitalized for a week each time she had a session of chemo. She had an IV inserted in her arm and the chemo was given on a slow drip that took four to five days to completely enter her system. And then she would come home for three weeks and then had to go back into the hospital for a week to get the next session of chemo.

In total, Mom had to complete six sessions of chemotherapy. Each session took a month to complete, so we knew that it would take six months for Mom to complete her chemotherapy. In fact, we liked the idea of giving the chemo to Mom on a slow drip, so it would not overwhelm her system. However, even on a slow drip, the chemo still proved to be overwhelming. You see, the chemo was destroying both the cancerous cells and her good cells as well.

After about the second session, Mom came home, and we could tell that the chemo was weakening her body. She didn't have much of an appetite. Also, when I would do her hair it was coming out in my hand. In addition, her skin had gotten darker and looked as if she was burnt.

Mom would be home for three weeks after a session of chemo. At the end of the third week, you could see that she was regaining some of strength back only to have to go back into the hospital to get the next session to be knocked down again. This was her third session, after it, Mom came home, and she was really weak, and her body was frail. All she could do was pretty much lay in the bed.

My brother said, "We are stopping this chemo, it's making Mom too weak. She can't even get up out of the bed, we are stopping it."

So, I said, "We are going to do what Mom wants to do she's not incapacitated and she can say what she wants to be done."

I went to my mom while she was in bed and I said, "Mom, it looks like this chemo is taking a toll on you. You're so weak and frail, so if you want to stop the chemo we can have it stopped. You had three sessions and you got three more sessions to go. So, just tell me what you want us to do."

My mom was laying in the bed and her body was so weak. If she would have tried to stand up by herself, she would have fallen down. She was so frail, her skin was darkened, and her hair was completely gone. It was so hard seeing my mom in this condition.

I said again, "So Mom, we can stop it if you want."

My mom looked up at me and said, "NO, I'm not stopping. **I'M PRESSING ON.**"

Therefore, I told the rest of the family what Mom said, she's not stopping and that she's **Pressing On**.

I continued, "so, all we got to do now is Press On with her because we are not stopping the chemo."

We stayed with Mom around the clock; at no time was she ever at home by herself. We all took turns caring for Mom. We set up a schedule for each person for every day of the week.

Those next three sessions were not easy by any stretch of the imagination. The nurse would come to the house to check Mom's vitals and give her a needle in her thigh to help boost her good cells. She told us that on the days she wasn't there, someone else would have to give her the needle. The nurse said she would teach one of us how to give Mom the needle.

I said, "Oh no, I don't think I can do that; I can't even look at the needle going in my arm when I have to get blood drawn. So, I'm not a good candidate for that. See if you can teach my brother how to do it."

So, my brother Tomie said, "Yes, teach me how to give my mom the shot and I'll do it."

I was so thankful that my brother was there every day to give Mom the needle in her thigh and I would say, "Alright Dr. Scott."

During those last three sessions Mom had to be rushed to the hospital by ambulance on at least two occasions. The entire year of 2006 was one of the hardest times of my life. I was on autopilot the entire year, not even thinking about what has to be done. You're just thrust into a place where you just do it.

The six sessions of chemotherapy are finally completed, and mom's body can rest a bit and build back up from being knocked down by the chemo. So, after about one month, after the last session of chemo it's time for the third step in this process which is RADIATION.

Radiation Treatment

Mom had to go to the hospital every day for five weeks to get radiation treatments. The radiation wasn't bad, in fact, I think in this entire process the radiation was the easiest and most non-evasive on her body. Therefore, for five weeks Mom didn't miss a day getting the radiation treatments. It took almost the entire year of 2006 to complete this process and Mom did it. She hung in there by the Grace and Mercy of God.

Praise God from Whom All Blessings Flow

Mom's hair grew back, her skin color came back to normal, and she regained some of the weight that she had lost during this year long process. So, I am thankful and happy to say that Mom has been cancer free now for 12 years and she is doing great!

You can find Mom these days at home enjoying our family, her children, grandchildren, and great-grandchildren. She still loves to travel, shop, and go on day trips.

During the day between the hours of 12:30 p.m. and 2:00 p.m., do not call Mom because she will be watching her stories, the Young and the Restless and the Bold and the Beautiful. She loves to watch her stories and if you're on the phone with her at this time she will not hear a word that you're saying because she will be concentrating on Victor & Nikki and Brooke & Ridge. I talk to Mom every day and part of our conversations is about what happened on the stories today.

August 2018 Mom's 90th Birthday

This August 2018, we will be celebrating Mom's 90th birthday. God has truly been a blessing to our family. I am so thankful, so humbled, and so grateful for God is my All in All, and without Him I am nothing. Thank You Jesus!! Glory be to God forever and ever, AMEN!

SURVIVOR OF CANCER
ELLEN SCOTT
HALL OF FAME HONOREE

MOM'S FAVORITE SCRIPTURE
(Psalm 121, 1-8-KJV)

1: I will lift up mine eyes unto the hills, from whence cometh my help.

2: My help cometh from the LORD, which made heaven and earth.

3: He will not suffer thy foot to be moved: he that keepeth thee will not slumber.

4: Behold, he that keepeth Israel shall neither slumber nor sleep.

5: The LORD is thy keeper: the LORD is thy shade upon thy right hand.

6: The sun shall not smite thee by day, nor the moon by night.

7: The LORD shall preserve thee from all evil: he shall preserve thy soul.

8: The LORD shall preserve thy going out and thy coming in from this time forth, and even for evermore.

MOM, YOU KEEP PRESSING ON!

Mom, you are so **Very Strong**

And NO MATTER what **Storms**

That may come your Way

You Keep Pressing On!

You Press On,

Until the Issue you're facing

Is **Resolved or Gone**

Mom, you KEEP **Moving Forward**

With your **Eyes Looking Upward**

Upward Towards the Hills

Which Cometh Your Help

And you **Look Upward**

Because of your **Complete Trust in God**

And as your Family,

We see your **Courage**

And the **Deep Faith**

That's Inside

A **Faith** that NEVER **Wavers**

Because of your **Belief in The Creator**

And **His Favor**

Mom, you are a **Survivor**

Not just from **Cancer**

But a Survivor of Life

You **Survived Daily** by

Allowing God to Order your Steps

By Listening to **His Voice**

And **Following His Guidance**

You **Survived by Holding On**

And Refusing to **Let Go**

Even with the Loss of your Two Beloved Sons

Robert and Bo

Because You ALWAYS know...

That God will **Show you**

When you Awake

The **Right Decisions** and/or

What **Path to Take**

Mom,

You **Solely Believes** in **His Leading,**

As You're Pressing On

You Press On...

While Doing your **Best**

Feeling Confident and **Extremely Blessed**

For we know that **God**

WILL Definitely Do the Rest

Mom,

90 Years is a **True Testimony** Itself

A **Testimony** on how you have **Lived**

And **Survived these Years**

With God on Your Side

Mom,

You are an AWESOME **Mother**

And **Women of God**

And as a Family

Mom, we are **Proud** and **Thankful**

We are **Thankful**

That **God Chose** YOU as **Our Mother**

That you are **So Strong**

And that you **Are A Survivor**

MOST IMPORTANTLY,

MOM, YOU KEEP PRESSING ON!

Lovingly Submitted, The Scott Family

ABOUT THE AUTHOR

My name is Elizabeth Scott known to my family and friends as Liz. I am originally from Philadelphia, PA, where I grew up. And now resides in Dover, Delaware.

I have wanted to write a book for some time now but didn't know where to get started. There were many questions running through my mind; do I write fiction or non-fiction and exactly what do I write about? So, I prayed and asked the Lord to lead me in which way I should go. And He graciously laid it upon my heart to write the story of my mom. Because she is both inspirational and a survivor. So, it is written in love and in her honor. I pray this book will inspire and encourage you, that you too can be a survivor of life. That is my mother's testimony and this book will show you how to **KEEP PRESSING ON**!

www.ingramcontent.com/pod-product-compliance
Lightning Source LLC
Chambersburg PA
CBHW052117070526
44584CB00017B/2530